HOMES
AROUND THE WORLD

by
Joanna Brundle

Look for red words in this book. You can find out what they mean in the Glossary on Page 24.

CONTENTS

We are going to visit lots of countries. Look at the map on page 22-23 to find out where they are.

©2016
Book Life
King's Lynn
Norfolk PE30 4LS

ISBN: 978-1-78637-010-5

Written by:
Joanna Brundle

Designed by:
Drue Rintoul

A catalogue record for this book is available from the British Library.

WHAT IS A HOME?

A home is a place where somebody lives. There are lots of different kinds of homes around the world.

A home is a place to eat, to sleep and to play. It protects us from rain, wind, snow and sun.

WHAT ARE HOMES MADE OF?

This home in India is made of wood. The roof is made of thatch, which is dried reeds or grasses tied together.

THATCH

WOOD

Your home is probably made of bricks, with tiles on the roof.

Stones have been used to build this home in Lesotho.

These homes in Turkey are made of clay.

HOMES IN THE COUNTRYSIDE

Some people live in homes in the countryside.

A COUNTRYSIDE HOME WITH A GARDEN IN UKRAINE.

This farmhouse in Russia has lots of space around it for animals to graze.

HOMES IN TOWNS AND CITIES

Homes in towns and cities are often very close together.

THERE IS NO ROOM FOR ANYONE ELSE IN THESE HOMES IN HONG KONG!

Many people in towns and cities live in flats or town houses. Often they have no garden.

TOWN HOUSES IN LONDON

WHERE ELSE DO PEOPLE LIVE?

Some homes are in the mountains, on the beach or by a lake. This wooden home in Canada is built from the pine trees which grow around it.

PINE TREES

CANADA

In Cambodia, homes, schools and shops float on Tonle Sap lake.

This home in the trees is in Thailand.

13

CITY SLUMS

Many people who live in cities around the world are very poor. They live in areas called slums.

SLUMS IN RIO, BRAZIL ARE CALLED FAVELAS.

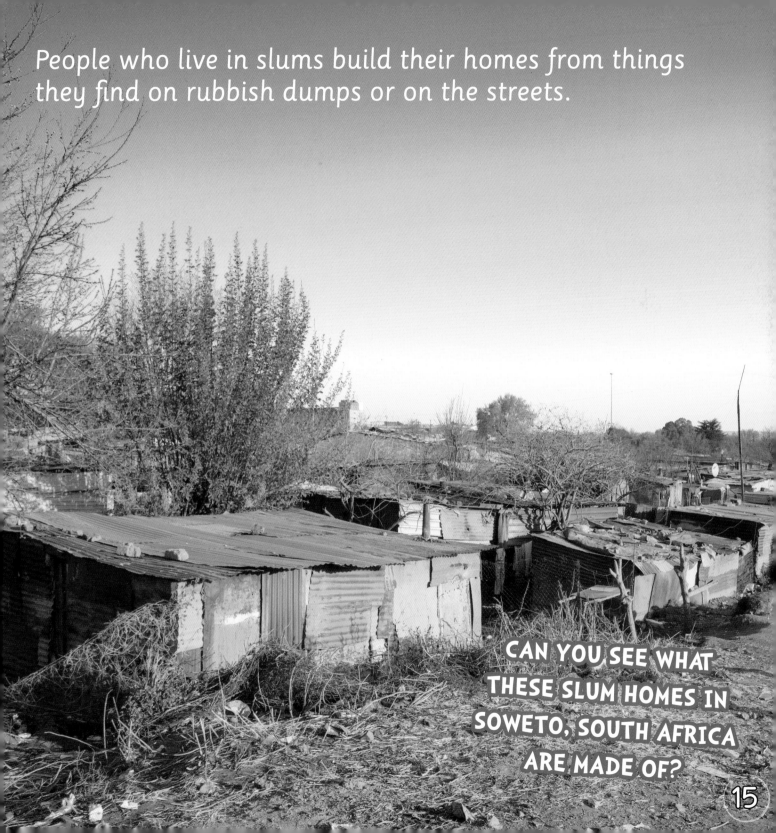

People who live in slums build their homes from things they find on rubbish dumps or on the streets.

CAN YOU SEE WHAT THESE SLUM HOMES IN SOWETO, SOUTH AFRICA ARE MADE OF?

15

UNUSUAL HOMES

Some people make their homes in unusual places.

THIS HOME IN PORTUGAL HAS BEEN BUILT BETWEEN TWO HUGE ROCKS.

An igloo gives shelter in snowy countries like Iceland.

A family have made their home in this lighthouse in The Netherlands.

HUTS, CAVES AND TENTS

In Namibia, the Himba people live in huts made of dried mud.

These caves are home to some people in Turkey.

A tent is home to these refugees from Syria.

HOMES ON THE MOVE

Some people move from place to place and take their homes with them.

THESE YURTS TRAVEL WITH THE FAMILY IN MONGOLIA.

When your home is a boat or caravan, you can travel where you like.

HOUSEBOAT IN THE UNITED KINGDOM

ROMANY CARAVAN

WHERE IN THE WORLD?

1. Brazil
2. Cambodia
3. Canada
4. Hong Kong
5. Iceland
6. India
7. Lesotho
8. Mongolia
9. Namibia
10. The Netherlands
11. Portugal
12. Russia
13. South Africa
14. Syria
15. Thailand
16. Turkey
17. Ukraine
18. UK

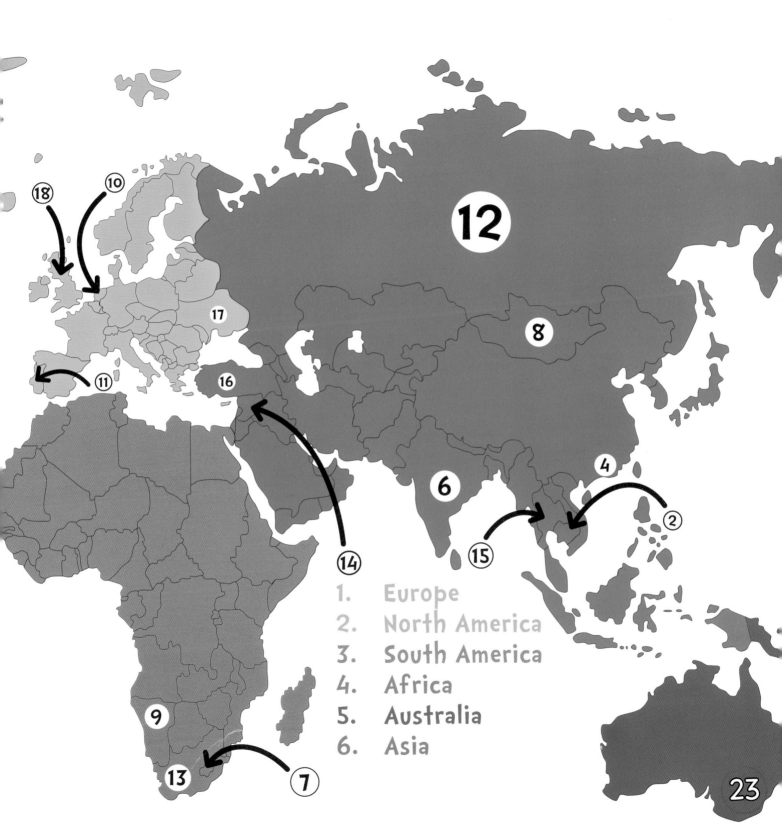

1. Europe
2. North America
3. South America
4. Africa
5. Australia
6. Asia

23

GLOSSARY

CLAY A sticky natural material that dries hard

GRAZE Eat grass in a field

REFUGEES People who have been forced to leave homes in their own country to escape from danger

ROMANY A person who belongs to a group of people who travel through Europe by caravan

SLUMS Areas on the edge of cities, where very poor people live in dirty conditions

YURTS Tents that can be moved, made of a wooden frame and sometimes covered in animal skins

INDEX

Photocredits: Abbreviations: l–left, r–right, b–bottom, t–top, c–centre, m–middle. All images are courtesy of Shutterstock.com.

2 – Dennis van de Wate. 4 – GuoZhongHua. 5 – Monkey Business Images. 6bl – RTimages. 6m – Michel Piccaya. 7m – Valery Shanin. 7tl – meunierd. 8 – Iryna Rasko. 9 – joyfull. 10 – leungchopan. 11 – Ron Ellis. 12 – Don Mammoser. 13m – Kushch Dmitry. 13bl – Mrs_ya. 14 – Ronaldo Almeida. 15 – Gil.K. 16 – StockPhotosArt. 17m – T.W. van Urk. 17tr – Vitalii_Mamchuk. 18 – Planetphoto.ch. 19m – Tracing Tea. 19bl – thomas koch. 20 – Tan Kian Khoon. 21m – StockCube. 21bl – PhillipsC. 22,23 – Milne.